FATHER CHRISTMAS'
JOKE BOOK

FATHER CHRISTMAS'
JOKE BOOK

Terry Deary

Illustrated by Stuart Trotter

Hippo Books
Scholastic Publications Limited
London

Scholastic Publications Ltd.,
10 Earlham Street, London WC2H 9RX, UK

Scholastic Inc.,
730 Broadway, New York, NY 10003, USA

Scholastic Canada Ltd.,
123 Newkirk Road, Richmond Hill,
Ontario L4C 3G5, Canada

Ashton Scholastic Pty Ltd.,
P O Box 579, Gosford, New South Wales,
Australia

Ashton Scholastic Ltd.,
165 Marua Road, Panmure, Auckland 6,
New Zealand

Published by Scholastic Publications Ltd., 1990

Copyright © Terry Deary
Illustration copyright © Stuart Trotter

ISBN 0 590 76408 X

Typeset by AKM Associates (UK) Ltd., Southall, London
Printed by Cox and Wyman Ltd., Reading, Berks

Contents

Introduction   7
One Christmas Joke Book   10
Two Christmas Carols   16
Three Christmas Knockers   23
Four Christmas Presents   32
Five Christmas Crackers   46
Six Panto Tickets   54
Seven Greedy Gnomes   66
Eight Stuffed Turkeys   72
Nine Christmas Puzzles   83
Ten Christmas Stories   94
Eleven Christmas Jokes   109
Twelve Father Christmases   127

Introduction

Me name is Father Christmas,
Some call me Santa Claus,
I'm here to bring you joy, my friends,
At Christmas time, because
. . . it's me job.

I live up at the North Pole
With all me little gnomes.
They can be pests, but stay with me
'Cos they've no other homes
. . . to go to.

We spend the lovely summer days
Just making lots of toys.
Then Christmas Eve we dash around
And give them to all boys
. . . and girls.

But winter nights we sit around
A roaring, great log fire.
We then tell jokes and stories
Till our eyes and voices tire
. . . and we go to bed.

A happy time we have then,
With jokes from all the gnomes,
But best of all they like to hear
The Father Christmas poems
. . . like this one.

One winter night Gnome Gnancy
Cried, "Hey, Father Christmas, look!
It's time we all sat down and wrote
These jokes up in a book
. . . for kids."

"A great idea that!" I agreed.
"Ho-ho! Ho-ho! Ho-ho!
I'll put in all me funny poems."
The gnomes all shouted "No!"
. . . but I have anyway.

So here's a book of Monster Laughs
And fun for Christmas time.
(I'd say "For all the family"
But can't think of a rhyme
. . . to go with family.)

So all the best at Christmas
Peace and goodwill to all.
And don't forget the mince pies
And the sherry when I call
. . . at your house to deliver all your presents.

ON THE FIRST DAY OF CHRISTMAS
MY TRUE LOVE SENT TO ME

ONE CHRISTMAS
JOKE BOOK

Hello!
*I'm a gnome and me name is Gnancy. Gnancy The
Gnome.*
*I'm one of Father Christmas' helpers. There are
seven of us who help him pack the presents and
deliver them every Christmas.*
First of all there's Gnorman The Gnome . . .

I wouldn't say Gnorman was small, but he used
to be a lumberjack on a mushroom farm!

GNORMAN   GNANCY

10

In fact, he's so small that he has to stand on a ladder to fasten his shoe laces!

Then there's Gnora The Gnome . . .

I wouldn't say Gnora was ugly, but if beauty's skin deep then she was born inside out!

I wouldn't say Gnora was cross-eyed, but when she cries the tears run down her back!

She'd make a terrible teacher – she has no control of her pupils!

Of course you must know Gnigel The Gnome. He's not too bright is Gnigel.

TEACHER: Gnigel! Give me a sentence with the word gnome in it!
GNIGEL: Er . . . the man's house burnt down so . . . he hadn't a gnome to go to!

GNORA

GNIGEL

Then there's Gnellie. She's always poorly . . .

GNELLIE: Doctor, doctor! I keep seeing pink and green spots in front of my eyes!

DOCTOR: Good gracious! Have you seen an optician?

GNELLIE: No . . . just pink and green spots!

DOCTOR: I mean, have you ever had your eyes checked?

GNELLIE: No. They've always been blue!

Or Gneil. You wouldn't be too keen on him! He's so mean!

FATHER CHRISTMAS: How do I stop Gneil being airsick on the sledge?

GNANCY: Put a five pound note between his teeth and stick his head over the side of the sledge.

GNELLIE

GNEIL

And you must have met Gnocker! He's always on the
wrong side of the front door . . .

Gnock! Gnock!
Who's there?
You.
You who?
Yoo-hoo! Nice to see you!

GNOCKER

13

Father Christmas is a jolly old chap. We have lots of happy jokes around Christmas time. You can always tell we're having a good time from the noise we make . . .

What goes "Ho! Ho! Ho! Thump!"?
Father Christmas laughing his head off!

We live at the North Pole, of course. Very cold, the North Pole.

"It's so cold outside," Gnora The Gnome said, "that I just watched a polar bear jump from one iceberg to another and it froze in mid-air!"

"That's impossible," Father Christmas said. "The law of gravity won't allow that!"

"Oh, I know," Gnora said, "but the law of gravity's frozen too!"

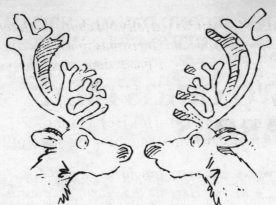

Only the reindeer can stand the cold . . .

"Father Christmas has two reindeer," Gnora the Gnome said. "He calls one Edward and the other one Edward! I bet you can't tell me why he does that!"

"Oh, yes I can," Gnorman the Gnome said. "Because two 'Eds are better than one, of course!"

And as the reindeer say before they tell you jokes . . .

These jokes will sleigh you!

So, be warned!!! Reading The Father Christmas Joke Book *can damage your brain cells . . . if you have any. And laughing can split your side – but if that happens just go for a fast run . . . you're sure to get a stitch in it!*

ON THE SECOND DAY OF CHRISTMAS
MY TRUE LOVE SENT TO ME

TWO CHRISTMAS CAROLS

Everybody has their favourite song at Christmas. What's yours? Here at the North Pole we have a favourite . . .

What song do Father Christmas' gnomes sing to him when he comes home cold on Christmas night?
Freeze a jolly good fellow!

But it's not just at the North Pole where they like their Christmas songs. In Africa they have them too . . .

GNORA:	What's Tarzan's favourite Christmas song?
GNORMAN:	Jungle bells, of course.
GNELLIE:	But what about his chimp?
GNEIL:	King Kong merrily on high, of course!

Not to mention the Sahara desert . . .

GNANCY:	So, what's the top of the desert pops at Christmas?
GNIGEL:	No-well, No-well!
GNORMAN:	The three wise men crossed the desert, didn't they? What did they sing?
GNEIL:	They sang, "Oh camel ye faithful!"
GNELLIE:	But what did the camels sing?
GNORA:	"All things bright and beautiful, All creatures grunt and smell!"

GNANCY: They didn't have camels. They had cars and sang,
"We three kings of Orient are
Driving off in our old cars;
One's a Ford and one's a Mini,
And one is a Jaguar."

GNORA: Rubbish! What they really sang was . . .
"We three Kings of Orient are
Trying to smoke a rubber cigar,
It was loaded with explosive . . .
BANG!!
Now we're with yonder stars!"

GNORMAN: So what did the shepherds sing, smarty pants?

GNORA: Everybody knows that!

18

"While shepherds washed their
socks by night
All seated by the tub
An angel of the Lord flew down
And gave them all a scrub!"

Of course Gnocker had to stick his oar in . . .

Gnock, Gnock!
Who's there?
Our Wayne!
Our Wayne who?
Our Wayne in a manger!

*But Gnocker The Gnome isn't so amused when
people come knocking on **his** door at midnight.*

19

Gnock, Gnock!
Who's there?
Carol singers!
Carol singers! Do you know what flaming time of night it is?
No. But if you hum it we'll sing it!

So do you know the favourite Christmas song of these people?

What's a hairdresser's favourite Christmas song?
"Oh comb all ye faithful"

A football supporter?
"Yule never walk alone"

Bugs Bunny?
"Lettuce with a gladsome mind"

A talkative princess in a tower?
"Silent Knight!"

Mind you, not everybody enjoys Christmas. Fairies
sing this sad ditty at Christmas time . . .

A fairy has a hard time,
Up where the tinsel flickers;
A wand of gold stuck in her hand,
A fir tree up her knickers!

And it isn't just fairies who have a bad time at
Christmas . . .

Oh little town 'neath moonlit skies
How still we see thee sleep.
As through the streets and on the roofs
A hooded figure creeps.
He climbs down all your chimneys
He carries a large sack . . .
He fills it with your valuables
Then quickly hurries back!

Now Gnora The Gnome is an awful singer . . . but,
alas, that doesn't stop her trying.

One night Gnora went carol singing. She
knocked on the door of a house and began to
sing. A man with a violin in his hand came to the

21

door. Within half a minute tears were streaming down his face! Gnora went on singing for half an hour, every carol she knew – and some she didn't. At last she stopped.

"I understand," she said softly. "You are remembering your happy childhood Christmas days. You're a sentimentalist!"

"No," he snivelled. "I'm a musician!"

But what is Father Christmas' favourite carol?

Father Christmas used to like "I'm dreaming of a quiet Christmas", but since we got a television at the North Pole he has a new favourite . . .
"Jingle Bells,
Batman smells,
Robin flew away.
The Batmobile has lost its wheels
Now it's a bat-mo-sleigh!"

22

THREE CHRISTMAS KNOCKERS

Did you know that Father Christmas' gnomes are afraid of Christmas?

GNIGEL: What do Gnomes fear most about Christmas?

GNOCKER: They're afraid Father Christmas will give them the sack!

Seriously, though, Father Christmas looks after us really well. It's not a lot of fun being a gnome. Especially if you're tiny like Gnorman.

GNORMAN: When I went to school I was hopeless at sport. In fact I once got lapped in the long jump! Everyone else was captain of the cricket or captain of the netball, captain of the rugby, captain of the football or captain of the swimming team. Teacher made me captain of the embroidery team!

23

GNIGEL: Before Father Christmas gave me a job I was offered work as a clown in a flea circus.

GNORA: Before Father Christmas gave me a job I was a novelist – but I was fed up with being called a "short" story writer.

GNORMAN: Before Father Christmas gave me a job I was a judge – but I got fed up with crooks saying, "These little things are sent to try us"!

GNELLIE: Before Father Christmas gave me a job I used to work as a body guard – to a dolls' house.

Gneil used to claim he was small but super-strong . . .

GNEIL: I'm so strong I could lift a reindeer with one hand.

GNORA: Yeah, but where are we going to find a one-handed reindeer?

But we all have our pets to keep us company . . .

GNIGEL: I have a dwarf elephant for a pet.

GNORA: What do you call a dwarf elephant?

GNIGEL: Trunk-ated!

GNORMAN:	What's that thing on your shoulder, Gneil?
GNEIL:	That's not a thing it's a newt!
GNORMAN:	What do you call him?
GNEIL:	I call him Tiny.
GNORMAN:	Why do you call him Tiny?
GNEIL:	Because he's my-newt!
GNELLIE:	Gnancy, what's that on your head?
GNANCY:	A sausage.
GNELLIE:	Is it your pet?
GNANCY:	No.
GNELLIE:	Is it to make you look taller?
GNANCY:	No.
GNELLIE:	So what is it?
GNANCY:	Why don't you ask it?
GNELLIE:	Sausage? What are you doing on Gnancy's head?
SAUSAGE:	I'm a head banger, of course!
GNOCKER:	Have you seen Gnancy's sausage? It looks like a Father Christmas or a hot dog.
GNIGEL:	A Father Christmas or a hot dog! What's the difference between a Father Christmas and a hot dog?
GNOCKER:	One wears a red suit . . . the other just pants.

And that reminds me. Gnocker knows all the worst jokes in the North Pole! Here are some of the best . . . you wouldn't want to hear the worst!

Gnock, Gnock!
Who's there?
Felix.
Felix who?
Felix-tremely cold at the North Pole.
SLAM!

Gnock! Gnock!
Who's there?
I'm just knocking to say your door-bell's broken!
I know – I want to be considered for a No-bel prize!

Gnock! Gnock!
Who's there?
Snow!
Snow White?
No. 'Snow place like home.
You fooled me there. SLAM!

Gnock! Gnock!
Who's there?
Icy!
Icy road?
No, I–cy you're still at home then.
Curses! I'm covered in silver paper!
Covered in silver paper?
Yes! I'm foiled again!

Gnock! Gnock!
Who's there?
Wooden shoe.
Wooden shoe who?
Wooden shoe like to know?
Not really! SLAM!

Gnock! Gnock!
Who's there?
Carol!
Christmas Carol?
No. Carol be parked in the garage.
They get worse. SLAM!

Gnock! Gnock!
Who's there?
Ken!
Ken who?
Ken I come in?
Not if you tell awful jokes like that!
You'll let me in sooner or later.
No I won't. SLAM!

Gnock! Gnock!
Who's there?
Wendy.
Don't tell me . . . "Wendy red, red robin comes bob, bob bobbin' along"?
You've heard it.
Heard it? I wrote it! SLAM!

Gnock! Gnock!
Who's there?
Cook!
Cook who?
A cuckoo? In December?
SLAM!

Gnock! Gnock!
Who's there?
The famous Memory man!
The famous Memory man who?
Er . . . what was the question again?
SLAM!

30

Gnock! Gnock!
Who's there?
Butcher!
Butcher with the turkey?
No. Butcher name down here. I've got a Christmas present for you.
Oh! Do come in!
I told you!

Gnock! Gnock!
Who's there?
Ghost.
Well, don't spook till you're spooken to! SLAM!

*So, with a pest like Gnocker around you can see why there's only **one** answer to a knock on the door.*

FOUR CHRISTMAS PRESENTS

Christmas is the time for giving presents. And it's our job to help Father Christmas fill the sacks, load the sleigh and fly around the world delivering them. Being gnomes, we can get down to the places Father Christmas can't reach. We also get to read the letters to Father Christmas. And some people do ask for funny presents.

But not everyone gets what they expect . . .

> Dear Father Christmas,
>   I am neatly bald. This
> Christmas could you please
> send me something to keep
> my hair in.
>   Signed
>   E.G. Hedd.

FATHER CHRISTMAS:	Send him a paper bag.
GNEIL:	Send him a comb; I'll bet he never parts with it!

People don't just write to us for presents. They ask their parents too . . .

LITTLE GIRL:	Mammy, mammy! Can I have a puppy for Christmas?
MOTHER:	Certainly not. You can have turkey like everybody else!
LITTLE BOY:	Dad! Can I have a broken drum for Christmas?
DAD:	The best thing you could have asked for. You can't beat it!

LITTLE BOY:	Daddy, Daddy! Can I have a wombat for Christmas?
DAD:	What would you do with a wombat?
LITTLE BOY:	Play wom, of course, stupid!

Of course the shops can be very helpful at Christmas, even though they're so busy.

GNORMAN:	I don't understand why we can't have Christmas in July, when the shops aren't so crowded!

Shop assistants often help husbands and wives choose presents for each other . . .

MAN:	My wife would like an unusual watch.
ASSISTANT:	Certainly, sir. This one has insects in place of numbers.
MAN:	So how do you tell the time?
ASSISTANT:	Easy. Look! It's just coming up to fly past flea.

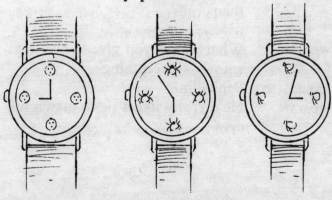

WOMAN:	Have you something for my husband? He has flat feet.
ASSISTANT:	Why not buy him a foot pump?
WOMAN:	And he suffers from water on the knee.
ASSISTANT:	So buy him some drainpipe trousers!
MAN:	I want some silk handkerchiefs for my wife.
ASSISTANT:	Certainly, sir. What size nose does she have?
MAN:	Actually she wanted something with diamonds but I only have two pounds.
ASSISTANT:	So, buy her a pack of cards.
MAN:	That train set looks fantastic. I'll take one.
ASSISTANT:	I'm sure your son will love it, sir!
MAN:	(sighs) Oh, yes . . . I suppose he would. You'd better give me two, then.
WOMAN:	What would you give to the man who has everything?
ASSISTANT:	Penicillin?
WOMAN:	He'd really like a tie to match his eyes.

ASSISTANT: Blue, brown, green or grey?

WOMAN: You don't do "bloodshot" I suppose?

Children can sometimes be very tiresome to buy presents for . . .

WOMAN: Excuse me, do you have a kitten for my little girl?

ASSISTANT: Sorry, madam, we don't do swaps.

WOMAN: I mean, have you got any kittens going cheap?

ASSISTANT: Certainly not! They all go miaow!

WOMAN: My son would like a snake.

ASSISTANT: We have a lovely boa constrictor.

WOMAN: He'd also like a Lego set.

ASSISTANT: So buy him a boa constructor!

MAN:	Do you have a pink car for my daughter?
ASSISTANT:	Sorry, sir, we're all sold out. It seems everyone in the country has bought a pink car this week.
MAN:	You realize what this means?
ASSISTANT:	Yes, sir. We're slowly turning into a pink car-nation!

MAN:	I'd like a magician's set for my son.
ASSISTANT:	Is he a beginner?
MAN:	No! He's been practising the sawing-people-in-half trick for years.
ASSISTANT:	Is he an only child?
MAN:	No, no! He has a lot of half-brothers and sisters.

Not everyone gets what they want for Christmas – or wants what they get . . . with millions of presents given every Christmas there are bound to be a few disappointments . . .

YOUNG MAN: Did you like the parrot I bought you darling? It sings, dances, tells jokes and recites poetry. What did you think of it?

GIRL: Well, to be honest, it was a bit tough, but the stuffing was nice.

WIFE:	Darling, you know that shock-proof, waterproof, anti-magnetic, un-breakable watch you bought me?
HUSBAND:	Yes, darling.
WIFE:	Well, it caught fire.
HUSBAND:	Good grief.
WIFE:	But it's all right. I threw it in the river to put it out.
HUSBAND:	It cost too much to throw away.
WIFE:	It's all right. I fished the watch out of the river and it's still running.
HUSBAND:	The watch is still running?
WIFE:	No. The river, stupid!

And even Scott of the Antarctic and Mrs Scott of the Antarctic had difficulty buying the right Christmas presents . . .

LITTLE BOY:	My Christmas stocking's got a hole in it.
FATHER:	Of course it has, dipstick. That's to get the presents in.
LITTLE BOY:	I asked for a hundred stocking fillers and all I got was this creepy crawly.
FATHER:	You *got* a hundred stocking fillers . . . that centipede has a hundred legs!
GIRL:	But I asked for a stereo radio. This isn't stereo.
MOTHER:	Yes it is. You just have to place your ears ten metres apart!

The real highlight of Christmas for us gnomes is Boxing Day when we get our own presents . . .

GNIGEL:	What did you get for Christmas, Gnancy?
GNANCY:	A mystery book.
GNIGEL:	What's it called?
GNANCY:	*The Case of the Stolen Chestnut* by Nick McConker.
GNELLIE:	I hear Ugly Gnora Gnome got a mud pack to make her more beautiful!

44

GNORMAN:	She did.
GNELLIE:	Did it work?
GNORMAN:	It really improved her appearance for three days.
GNELLIE:	Then what went wrong?
GNORMAN:	The mud fell off.

GNELLIE:	Gnora reckons she has the face of a sixteen-year-old girl!
GNORMAN:	She had – but we made her give it back!

FIVE CHRISTMAS CRACKERS

When we have our Christmas dinner we pull our crackers, put on the paper hats . . . and then we read the cracker jokes!

GNORA:	Why did the chicken cross the football pitch?
GNELLIE:	Because the referee whistled for a fowl!
GNORMAN:	What drink do frogs like best?
GNANCY:	Croaker-cola!

GNIGEL:	What do you get if you cross a kangaroo with an octopus, a sheep and a zebra?
GNOCKER:	A striped, woolly jumper with eight sleeves!
GNEIL:	Did you hear about the stupid plastic surgeon?
GNIGEL:	Yes. He stood in front of the fire and melted!
GNORMAN:	What time is it when you see an elephant sitting on your television?
GNORA:	Time to get a new television!
GNANCY:	Father Christmas lost his umbrella but he didn't get wet! Why not?
GNELLIE:	Because it wasn't raining!
GNIGEL:	Why can't a bike stand up by itself?
GNEIL:	Because it's two-tyred!

Some of the cracker jokes are very old . . .

I say, I say, I say! My wife's gone to the West Indies!
Jamaica?
No. She was quite happy to go!

47

GNELLIE: What do you get if you cross a whale with a bird that quacks?

GNANCY: Moby Duck!

GNORMAN: How do witches tell the time?

GNELLIE: With a witch-watch!

GNORMAN: What do you do if your dog has ticks?

GNORA: Don't wind him up!

GNEIL: How can you get your name in lights the world over?

GNIGEL: Change your name to Emergency Exit!

48

GNANCY: What do you get if you cross a gnome with a vampire?

GNORMAN: A monster that sucks the blood out of your kneecaps!

GNORMAN: Doctor, Doctor! Everyone thinks I'm a liar!

DOCTOR: I don't believe you!

GNOCKER: What flower can you eat?

GNELLIE: A cauli-flower!

Gnock! Gnock!
Who's there?
Dishes!
Dishes who?
Dishes Father Christmas, so let me in!

49

GNORA: What's the best way to catch a rabbit?

GNELLIE: Hide behind a bush and make a sound like a carrot!

GNANCY: How do you start a polar-bear race?

GNORMAN: Say "Ready! Teddy! Go!"

GNOCKER: Which animal should you *not* play cards with?

GNIGEL: A cheetah!

GNEIL: What do you get if you cross a hen with a bedside clock?

GNORA: An alarm cluck!

GNANCY: What would you do if a rhino charged you?

GNIGEL: Pay him!

GNOCKER: Why couldn't the sailors play cards?

GNORA: Because the captain was standing on the deck!

GNEIL: What do you get hanging from Father Christmas' roof?

GNIGEL: Tired arms!

GNORMAN:	I'm letting my pet pig sleep on my bed!
GNEIL:	What about the smell?
GNORMAN:	He'll just have to get used to it!
GNELLIE:	Why did mean Gneil buy a black and white dog?
GNANCY:	Because he'd heard that a black and white licence was cheaper.
GNORA:	Where are the Andes?
GNORMAN:	On the end of the armies!
GNELLIE:	What do you get if you cross a cowboy with an octopus?
GNANCY:	Billy the Squid.
GNORA:	Waiter! Waiter! My Christmas pudding is off!
WAITER:	Off? Where to?

GNEIL:	Who wrote the book, *The Awful Comedown*?
GNIGEL:	Lucy Lastick!
GNORMAN:	If I'm standing at the North Pole, facing the South Pole, and the East is on my left hand, what's on my right hand?
GNIGEL:	Fingers.
GNOCKER:	How do monkeys make toast?
GNORMAN:	Stick some bread under the gorilla!
GNOCKER:	What did the police do when the hares escaped from the zoo?
GNEIL:	They combed the area!
GNORMAN:	Why was the turkey in the pop group?
GNELLIE:	Because he was the only one with drum-sticks!

GNELLIE: How does Father Christmas climb up a chimney?

GNORA: He uses a ladder in the stocking!

GNORA: Why do you call your dog Metal-worker?

GNIGEL: Because every time he hears a knock he makes a bolt for the door.

GNOCKER: What song did Cinderella sing as she waited four months for her photos to come back from the chemist?

GNIGEL: "Some Day My Prints Will Come!"

ON THE SIXTH DAY OF CHRISTMAS
MY TRUE LOVE SENT TO ME

SIX PANTO TICKETS

The big Christmas treat for us gnomes is when Father Christmas takes us all to the theatre to see the pantomime. Of course, Father Christmas thinks he's too famous and popular to need tickets for the panto.

FATHER CHRISTMAS: (To box office girl) All right, my good lady, my face is my ticket.

BOX OFFICE ATTENDANT: Then you'd better watch out . . . there's a feller inside who has the job of punching the tickets!

Even the reindeer wanted to go to the panto –
so Father Christmas booked them into the
stalls.

Ghosts love to go to the theatre at Christmas –
they like to watch a good phantomime!

*Mind you, going to the theatre with Father
Christmas can be a bit embarrassing. He's forever
popping out to get an ice-cream – and he's far too fat
to squeeze back in.*

FATHER CHRISTMAS:	(To lady with a feathered hat) Excuse me, but did I step on your toes on my way out to get an ice-cream?
LADY:	You certainly did!
FATHER CHRISTMAS:	Oh good! That means I'm back in the right row!

*And you see such funny characters at the panto-
mime . . .*

GNELLIE:	Who's that little girl who wears a red cape and goes round shouting "Knickers" at the Big Bad Wolf?
FATHER CHRISTMAS:	That's Little Rude Riding Hood.

GNEIL:	I wouldn't let that Cinderella play on *my* hockey team.
FATHER CHRISTMAS:	Why not?
GNEIL:	'Cos she keeps running away from the ball!

The pantomime we went to see this year had all the usual characters. First there was the "Dame" . . . but she looked an awful lot like a man dressed up to me!

The pantomime dame was called old Mother Hubbard. She had her song, of course:

Old Mother Hubbard
Went to the cupboard
To get her poor doggy a bone.
When she got there
The cupboard was bare
So the dog bit her leg.

OLD MOTHER HUBBARD.   GRETEL RED RIDING HOOD.   PRINCE HANSEL.   BARON STONEY BROKE.   HELMUT HARDKNUT.

Now old Mother Hubbard's daughter was called Gretel and she had this red hood for riding. So she was known as Gretel Red Riding Hood. One day Old Mother Hubbard sent Gretel Red Riding Hood on an errand . . .

I WANT YOU TO VISIT GRANNY IN HER FOREST COTTAGE. SHE'S ILL.

POOR GRAN! PERHAPS I SHOULD TAKE HER SOME GOOD, WHOLESOME FOOD!

FOOD! FOOD! WHERE WILL WE GET FOOD? YOUR OLD MOTHER HUBBARD WENT TO THE CUPBOARD TO GET THE POOR DOGGY A BONE, BUT WHEN SHE GOT THERE THE CUPBOARD WAS SO BARE EVEN THE MICE HAD MOVED OUT. OH GRETEL RED RIDING HOOD, IF ONLY YOUR FATHER, ROBIN HOOD WERE ALIVE.

AH, YES, I WISH I'D KNOWN HIM. I'VE HEARD SO MUCH ABOUT HIM. HE USED TO ROB THE RICH TO GIVE TO THE POOR, DIDN'T HE?

NOT EXACTLY. HE USED TO ROB THE RICH 'COS THE POOR HAD NOTHING WORTH PINCHING!

And off our heroine went to Granny's cottage. Then the villain arrived. There's always a villain in a pantomime. In this one it was evil Baron Stoneybroke and his nasty henchman, Helmut Hardknut.

59

60

61

But then handsome Prince Hansel came on the scene. He was in disguise of course. In fact he looked a lot like a woman, just as Old Mother Hubbard looked a lot like a man. Very confusing, pantomimes. Even more confusing was Gretel Red Riding Hood in the forest. With Helmut Hardknut disguised as a wolf to catch her the only help she had was from the talking trees . . . whoever heard of a talking tree? Gretel Red Riding Hood hadn't at first!

And the panto ended with Old Mother Hubbard marrying Baron Stoneybroke, with Prince Hansel marrying Gretel Red Riding Hood . . .

and with Helmut Hardknut being arrested . . .

I ARREST YOU IN THE NAME OF THE FOREST LAW.

YOU CAN'T DO THAT! YOU'RE NOT A POLICEMAN.

OH YES I AM — I'M FROM SPECIAL BRANCH!

And of course everyone lived HAPPILY EVER AFTER!

SEVEN GREEDY GNOMES

Of course Gneil wouldn't go to a pantomime in case someone asked him to buy an ice-cream.

GNIGEL: What's Gneil's favourite Christmas game?

GNORA: Mean-opoly, of course!

GNORMAN: Someone bought Gneil a clock for Christmas. He put it straight in the bank.

GNELLIE: Why did he do that?

GNORMAN: He was trying to save time!

GNOCKER: But he broke his clock, didn't he?

GNANCY: That's right. He punched it.

GNOCKER: Why did he do that?

GNANCY: He said it was self-defence. He said the clock struck first!

Mind you, Gneil doesn't like to be called "mean". He says it all started with his dad . . .

66

GNEIL:	My dad was so mean he wouldn't let me have a sledge. He told me to slide down the hill on my little brother.
GNELLIE:	And Gneil's dad was too mean to pay for his swimming lessons. He just took Gneil down to the river and threw him in. It didn't work. Gneil kept getting out of the sack.

But all of Gneil's family are like that . . .

Gneil's family have the tidiest weddings the North Pole has ever seen . . . that's because all the confetti is on elastic.

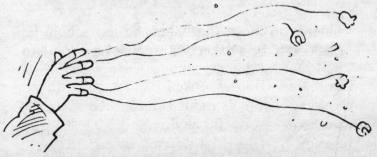

Some carol singers called at Gneil's house and said they were collecting for the local orphanage . . . so Gneil's mum gave them a couple of orphans!

Gneil's uncle was always burgling houses. He used to take a shower when he'd finished filling his sack with loot – so he could make a clean getaway!

He was once caught stealing a stop watch – but the judge gave him a second chance.

So that's why Gneil is the way he is.

Gneil's so mean that he has a lock on his dustbin.

Gneil's so mean that when he takes 10p out of his purse the Queen blinks in the light.

Gneil's so mean that he wakes up in the night to see if he's lost any sleep.

Gneil's so mean that when he left school he decided to be a baker . . . because he wanted to make lots of dough.

Gneil's so mean that he once found a pair of crutches and broke both of his legs so that he could use them!

Now there are lots of stories about Gneil's meanness. Like when he was at school . . .

TEACHER: Tell me, Gnellie, if I have 20p and ask Gneil for another 30p how much will I have?
GNELLIE: Please, miss, 20p!
TEACHER: Gnellie, you don't know your arithmetic.
GNELLIE: Please, miss, you don't know your Gneil!

Gneil bought the cheapest canoe he could get to paddle round the Arctic Sea. It was so cheap it had no heater. One day he was freezing cold so he broke off some of the wood at the front and started a little fire in the cockpit of his kayak. That warmed him up a bit so he broke off some more. Soon there was only half his kayak left . . . and the first wave that came along sank him. Father Christmas had to rescue him and gave him a good telling off.

"Let that be a lesson to you, Gneil!"

"I know, I know!" the poor gnome moaned. "Don't tell me! I can't half my kayak and heat it!"

One day Gneil went up to Father Christmas and said, "Tell me, Father Christmas, are you superstitious?"

"Not at all," Father Christmas replied.

"Good," Gneil said. "Then will you lend me £13 please?"

Gneil was always trying to borrow money, of course. But there was one time when he offered some . . .

One summer Father Christmas decided to go for a holiday in the Canary Islands. (He'd heard they were cheap!) He'd just finished packing the sledge when Gnellie told him that there was no snow in the Canary Islands. The sledge wouldn't go!

"What shall I do?" Father Christmas asked.

"Well," Gnellie replied, "my brother has a Porsche for sale . . ."

"I've got one on the front of my house," Father Christmas said.

"No, Father Christmas, I said a Porsche, not a porch . . . it's a car. Anyway, he's selling it for twenty thousand pounds – it's a bargain!" Gnellie explained.

So Father Christmas went to his piggy bank, broke it open and took out his money. "Oh, dear!" he moaned. "I've only got nineteen-thousand, nine-hundred and ninety-nine pounds and ninety pence! What shall I do?"

He dashed to the front door and saw Gneil walking down the road outside. "Gneil! Gneil!" Father Christmas cried. "Can you give me ten pence to buy a Porsche?"

Gneil's greedy little eyes lit up! "Certainly, Father Christmas!" he grinned. "Here's *twenty* pence – get me one too!"

ON THE EIGHTH DAY OF CHRISTMAS
MY TRUE LOVE SENT TO ME

EIGHT STUFFED TURKEYS

Christmas is a time for eating and drinking – even at the North Pole . . .

Father Christmas and the seven gnomes don't have a turkey for Christmas, they have an octopus . . . it doesn't taste half as nice, but at least everyone gets a leg!

To tell the truth, turkeys are a bit expensive. Father Christmas went to a butcher's and saw that the turkeys were 90p a pound. He said to the butcher, "Do you raise them yourself?"

"Of course I do," the butcher replied. "They were only 50p a pound this morning!"

Gnigel's mother bought a huge turkey. "That must have cost a fortune!" Gnigel cried. "Actually I got it for a poultry amount," she said.

We're usually too busy to cook our own Christmas dinner at that time of the year. We always end up eating at the "Greasy Penguin Cafe". There's a sign that says: "The Greasy Penguin – Eat Dirt Cheap" . . . but, as Gneil says, "Who wants to eat dirt?"

It's in The Good Food Guide to Christmas Breakfasts *by Egall Runney.*

It's also the only place in the North Pole where the dustbins have indigestion.

We always start with the soup . . .

FATHER CHRISTMAS:	Waiter! Waiter! There's a spider in my soup!
WAITER:	Sorry, sir, it's the fly's day off.
GNORMAN:	Waiter! Waiter! There's a caterpillar on my Christmas dinner.
WAITER:	That's all right, mate, caterpillars don't eat much!

GNELLIE: Waiter! Waiter! There's a fly in the butter!

WAITER: Yes, miss, it's a butter-fly.

GNORA: Waiter! Waiter! Why is this biscuit crying?

WAITER: Ah, miss, that's 'cos its mum's been a wafer too long.

GNANCY: Waiter! Waiter! Can you make a sandwich spread?

WAITER: Yeah! I'll just sit on it.

GNEIL: Waiter! Waiter! This soup's expensive.

WAITER: What do you expect? It's 24 carrot soup!

GNOCKER: Waiter! Waiter! These chicken legs have no knees!

WAITER: Yes that's because it's a cock chicken. You'd have to go to London for the knees.

GNOCKER: Why?

WAITER: Because all the cock-knees are in London.

GNORMAN: Waiter! Waiter! This turkey tastes like an old settee.

WAITER:	Well, you asked for something with plenty of stuffing.
GNORMAN:	But it's tough!
WAITER:	(Trying a piece) Tastes tender enough to me!
GNORMAN:	It should be! I've just chewed that bit for twenty minutes!
FATHER CHRISTMAS:	I wanted a whole turkey. This one only has one leg!
WAITER:	Perhaps it's been in a fight.
FATHER CHRISTMAS:	Well take it back and bring me the winner!

GNEIL: Waiter! Waiter! This turkey's disgusting!

WAITER: Well, you asked for a foul roast, didn't you?

GNANCY: Waiter! Waiter! I'll bet even a turkey wouldn't drink the coffee here!

WAITER: Of course not . . . it would go to a Nest-cafe.

GNORMAN: This turkey's fit for nothing.

WAITER: A tur-key's always good for something.

GNORMAN: What?

WAITER: Opening Turkish doors.

GNORA: Waiter! Waiter! Bring me a crocodile sandwich and make it snappy!

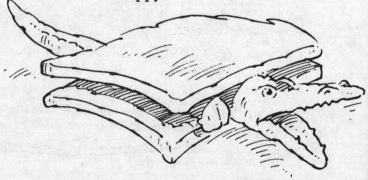

WAITER: And would you like some fast vegetables with it?

GNORA: What are your fastest vegetables?

WAITER: Runner beans, of course.

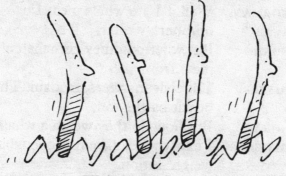

GNOCKER: Waiter! Waiter! Bring me an omelette.

WAITER: Would you like a French or a Spanish omelette?

GNOCKER: I don't mind . . . I want to eat it not talk to it!

GNEIL: Waiter! Waiter! This lemon is damaged.

WAITER: Don't worry, it just needs some lemon-aid.

GNELLIE: Waiter! Waiter! Is that policeman over there eating turkey?

WAITER: No, madam . . . he's eating truncheon meat.

GNORMAN: Waiter! Waiter! Is that Eskimo over there eating turkey?

WAITER: No, sir. Eskimos eat whale meat and blubber.

GNORMAN: Well if I ate whale meat I'd blubber.

GNORA: But where do they get whale meat from?

WAITER: The fish-mongers, madam. They buy it by the ton.

GNORA: But how do they weigh a whale?

WAITER: I expect they take it to the whale-weigh station.

GNORMAN: Waiter! Waiter! This stuffing is odd. It's sausage meat at one end – but the other end is bread.

WAITER: I know, sir. We're short of money at the moment. The manager's having trouble making both ends meat.

GNANCY: Waiter! Waiter! I'd like Father Christmas stew.

WAITER: Er . . . how do you make Father Christmas stew?

GNANCY: You keep him waiting half an hour!

FATHER CHRISTMAS:	Last year's Christmas pudding was so awful I threw it in the ocean.
WAITER:	That's probably why the ocean's full of currants!

GNOCKER:	But, waiter, what's the best way to keep a pudding?
WAITER:	Don't eat it.
GNELLIE:	Waiter! Waiter! Could you bring me some double cream for my pudding?
WAITER:	No double cream, sorry. Will two singles do?

GNORMAN: Who made this Christmas pudding?

WAITER: Our chef. He's a little green man who lives in a toadstool.

GNORMAN: What did he use to make it?

WAITER: Elf-raising flour, of course.

GNIGEL: Waiter! Waiter! Have you ever tasted turkey soup?

WAITER: Turkey's soup? I've never met a turkey who could cook! The only turkeys we had here had terrible manners.

GNIGEL: They did?

WAITER: Yes, sir. They used to gobble at the table.

*If you want to see someone with **real** problems at Christmas, then look at a turkey . . .*

Did you hear about the stupid turkey?
It was looking forward to Christmas!

Why did the turkey cross the road?
To prove it wasn't chicken.

And why did the one-eyed turkey cross the road?
To get to the Bird's Eye shop.

What's a turkey's favourite television programme?
A duckumentary!

How can you tell an owl's wiser than a chicken?
Well, did you ever hear of Kentucky Fried
owl?

How do you tell the difference between tinned
turkey and tinned custard?
Look at the labels!

What do you get if you pour boiling water
down a rabbit hole?
Hot cross bunnies, of course.

ON THE NINTH DAY OF CHRISTMAS
MY TRUE LOVE SENT TO ME

NINE CHRISTMAS PUZZLES

At the North Pole we seven gnomes fight over the Christmas puzzle books to see if we can catch one another out . . . everyone except Gnigel who sleeps under the bed because he's a little potty . . . Anyway, see if you can work out the following puzzles. The answers are on page 92.

Riddles

1. What travels over water, under water but doesn't touch water?

2. How do you get down from an elephant?

3. If there are two flies in an airing cupboard, which one is in the army?

4. What is 96 years old, walks with a stick and lives at the North Pole?

5. What tool do you use to flatten a ghost?

WRITE YOUR ANSWERS HERE.

1. _____

2. _____

3. _____

4. _____

5. _____

84

Word-search
6. Find the word that describes Father Christmas when he can't find his thermal knickers on Christmas morning.

```
G   R   U   M   P   Y
x   N   A   S   T   Y
F   U   R   I   O   U
A   N   G   R   Y   S
F   I   E   R   C   E
S   N   A   P   P   Y
```

7.

Spot the difference 1.

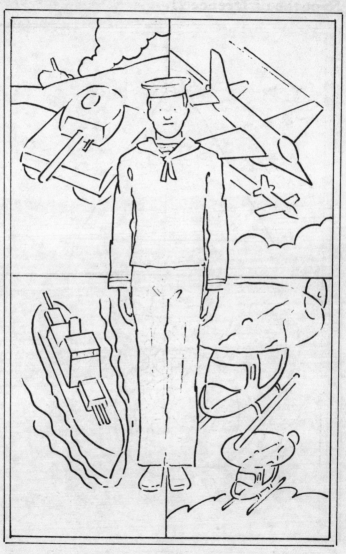

8.
Spot the difference 2.

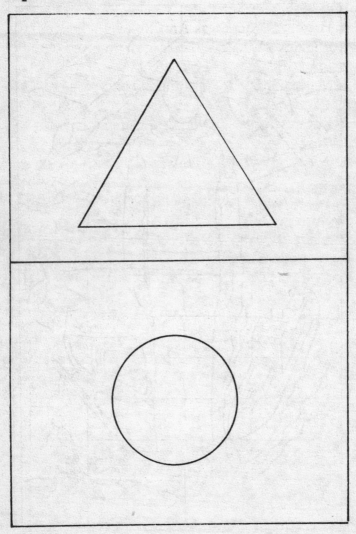

Test your knowledge

9. General Knowledge: Name three foods that begin with 't'.

10. History: Where was Ann Boleyn beheaded?

11. Biology: What is the largest mouse in the world?

12. Mathematics: If 2's company and 3's a crowd what are 4 and 5?

13. Physics: What do you call a snowman with a sun tan?

14. Geography: Where was King Solomon's temple?

15. Christmas: How many 'A' levels has Father Christmas got?

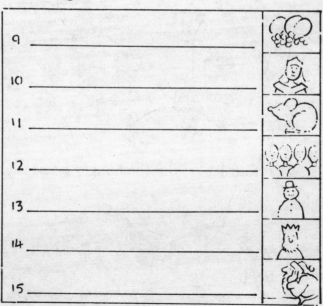

9 _____

10 _____

11 _____

12 _____

13 _____

14 _____

15 _____

Test your brain power

16. What seven letters did Father Christmas say when he looked in Gnigel's earhole?

17. What two letters did Father Christmas say when he looked at Gnora's rotten tooth?

18. What four letters did the hungry horse say?

Master-mind bender

19. Thirty days hath September, April, June and November, all the rest have thirty-one *but* ... how many months have twenty-eight days?

AND NOW, TURN THE PAGE TO CHECK YOUR ANSWERS ...

Answers

Riddles:

1. A man on a bridge with a bucket of water on his head.
2. You don't get down from an elephant – you get it from a swan.
3. The one on the tank.
4. A little cold lady.
5. A spirit level.

Word-search:

6. The answer is "x" – because he's a little cross.

Spot the difference **1:**

7. The difference is that you can't dip a sailor in your soft-boiled egg.

Spot the difference **2:**

8. There is no difference; they are both pictures of Father Christmas' house in a snowstorm.

Test your knowledge:

9. Tin of plums, tin of peaches and tin of peas.
10. Just below the chin.
11. The hippo-poto-mouse.
12. Nine.
13. A puddle.
14. On his forehead.
15. None. He just has "Ho! Ho! Ho!" levels.

Test your brain-power:
16. O.I.C.U.R.M.T.
17. D.K.
18. If you said M.T.G.G. you'd be *wrong*! The answer is *nothing* – 'cos horses can't talk, stupid!

Master-mind-bender
19. They all have! Ho! Ho! Ho!

Now Check Your Score
20: Dirty rotten cheat! There were only nineteen questions.

10–19: Clever clogs.

1–9: Thicko!

0: Look out, Gnigel, someone out there's as dim as you!

TEN CHRISTMAS STORIES

When Christmas is over we gnomes like to sit around the fire and tell our favourite stories.

FATHER CHRISTMAS:	Gnigel, what's your favourite story?
GNIGEL:	Er . . . the one where the three creatures are scared of the Big Bad Wolf and they grow on trees!
FATHER CHRISTMAS:	Oh, you mean "The Three Little Figs".

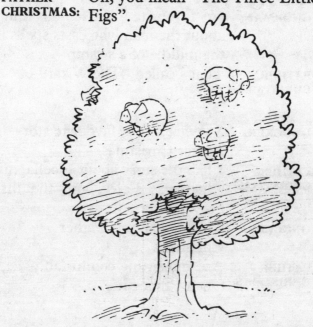

FATHER CHRISTMAS:	And what's your favourite Christmas story, Gneil?
GNEIL:	Oh, the one about the ghost that steals the porridge!
FATHER CHRISTMAS:	Oh, you mean "Ghoul-di-locks"!

GNELLIE:	I like the story about the girl who steals from the rich and gives it all to Granny.
FATHER CHRISTMAS:	Ah, that's "Little Red Robin Hood"!
GNORMAN:	My favourite is the famous film about the man who casts spells in the middle of a swamp.
FATHER CHRISTMAS:	That's called "The Wizard of Ooze"!
GNOCKER:	So what's your favourite story, Father Christmas?
FATHER CHRISTMAS:	I like the story about Floella, my Christmas Fairy, and the little brown hare.
GNOCKER:	Tell us that one, Father Christmas.
FATHER CHRISTMAS:	Are you sitting comfortably? Then I'll begin –

Once upon a time, in the Christmas Tree Forest there lived the Christmas fairies. They spent most of their time practising sitting on top of Christmas trees. There was just one rule they had to stick to . . . it was strictly forbidden for a fairy to kiss anyone!

The trouble was that Floella was a wicked little fairy.

One day Harry the Hare was hopping through the forest when he saw Floella sitting on top of a toadstool, combing her hair. Floella said, "Hello, handsome, give us a kiss!"

Harry the Hare was shocked. "Father Christmas doesn't allow it!" he gasped. "Anyone caught kissing a fairy will be turned straight away into a Goon!"

But Floella tickled his ears – just the way hares love – and whispered, "Don't worry, we won't be caught!"

Harry the Hare trembled with fear and excitement. He looked carefully over his furry brown shoulder, saw that no one was looking . . . and *kissed* Floella the fairy!

Suddenly there was a FLASH, a C*R*A*S*H and a mighty WHOOSH!!! of wind. Through the magic of the Christmas Tree Forest Harry the Hare found himself in the court of Father Christmas!

And Father Christmas was furious! "Harry the Hare! You have been found guilty of kissing a forest fairy! Have you anything to say?"

"I never meant to!" Harry the Hare snivelled. "If you let me off I promise I'll never do it again . . . just please, please!! PLEASE!!! don't turn me into a Goon!"

Father Christmas took pity on the pathetic creature and said, "I'll give you one more chance . . . just one more!"

Suddenly there was a FLASH, a C*R*A*S*H and a mighty WHOOSH!!! of wind. Harry the

Hare found himself back in the forest. And there, combing her hair on a toadstool was Floella the Fairy.

"Hiya, handsome," she whispered. "Give us a kiss!"

Harry the Hare was horrified! "Certainly not!" he cried. But when she tickled his ears his legs turned to jelly and he started to tremble. "Oooh! No! I'll be turned into a Goon!"

"For one little kiss from me it's worth it!" Floella murmured.

And Harry the Hare gave in. He kissed the fairy.

Suddenly there was a FLASH, a C*R*A*S*H and a mighty WHOOSH!!! of wind. Once again Harry the Hare found himself in front of the furious Father Christmas!

"You foolish hare!" Father Christmas roared. "You have had your chance! Guards! Take him away – turn him into a Goon tomorrow!"

Harry the Hare hung his head and let himself be led away. As he reached the door of the court he turned to all the gnomes and forest creatures and said tearfully . . .

"Ah, well, that's life! Hare today . . . and Goon tomorrow!"

Now Gnigel's favourite story was about Gneil . . .

One day Gnigel went for a walk to the North Pole to feed the penguins. Who should he meet there but Gneil! And Gneil had a sack of green and purple sand and he was scattering it all over the snow.

"Gneil! What on earth are you doing?" Gnigel asked.

"I'm scattering this magic green and purple sand," Gneil told him.

"But *why* are you scattering green and purple sand?" Gnigel demanded.

"To keep the crocodiles away, of course!" Gneil told him.

Gnigel gasped. "But there *aren't* any crocodiles at the North Pole!"

Gneil grinned happily. "I know. Great stuff
isn't it?"

*Gnora loved to hear a ghost story at Christmas. She
particularly loved the one about the ghostly dog . . .*

There was once a dog who died and came back
to haunt the street he lived in.

He loved scaring cats. One Christmas Eve, just about midnight, he'd scared a fat black moggy and sent it howling home. The ghost dog was so happy he wagged his ghost-tail and wagged his ghost-tail . . . until it dropped off!

The tail lay sadly on the ground. The dog picked it up in his mouth but couldn't reach behind to stick it back on. Midnight was striking and people were flocking to the pub that was open late. The dog wandered into the pub and jumped on to the bar.

"Excuse me," the dog said politely. "But do you think you could stick my tail back on?"

The landlord turned and looked at the clock on the wall behind the bar. "Oh, sorry mate," he sighed. "But, you see, I'm not permitted to re-tail spirits after midnight!"

Gnorman liked ghost stories too. But his favourite was about the Christmas wrapping string . . .

One Christmas Eve, when all the presents had been wrapped, there were just three pieces of string left.

"You know, we'll probably just be thrown on the fire," String No. 1 said.

"Or in the bin!" String No.2 moaned.

"We can't have that!" String No. 3 cried.

"So what can we do?" the other two pieces asked.

"Let's go out for a meal!" String No. 3 suggested.

And off they went down to the "Greasy Penguin Cafe". It was packed with Christmas revellers. String No. 1 said, "Right, lads, what'll we eat?"

"I'd like some tomato soup," said String No.2.

"And how about stuffed turkey to follow . . . and we could have Christmas pudding for afters," said String No. 3.

String No. 1 went to the counter and said, "Three tomato soups, three stuffed turkeys and three Christmas puddings, my good man!"

The waiter took one look at him and said, "Push off, shorty. I don't serve pieces of string . . . and you're just a piece of string!"

String No. 1 went back to the others. "He refused to serve me!"

String No. 2 asked, "Did you say 'please'?"

"No," admitted String No. 1.

"Then let me try!"

String No.2 went to the bar and said, "Three tomato soups, three stuffed turkeys and three Christmas puddings, *please*."

But the waiter replied, "Push off, shorty. I don't serve pieces of string . . . and you're just a piece of string!"

String No.2 went back to the others to report

his failure. "Here, lads, let me try," String No.3 offered. But, before he went to the bar he tied a knot in the top of his head and fluffed the end out till he looked like a piece of punk string.

He went up to the bar. "Three tomato soups, three stuffed turkeys and three Christmas puddings, please!"

The waiter looked at him and sighed, "Push off, shorty. I don't serve pieces of string . . . and you're just a piece of string!"

And String No.3 replied, "No. I'm a frayed knot!"

But Gnellie has my favourite Christmas story of all . . .

Once upon a time there was a little girl who wanted a kitten for Christmas. Now, her mother couldn't buy a kitten and parcel it up for Christmas Day, so she bought it a week before Christmas and gave it to the little girl. "You're getting your Christmas present a week early this year," her mother explained and handed over the fluffy little tabby kitten. "Is that what you want?"

The little girl, whose name was Kitty, said, "It's wonderful, mother . . . just what I wanted. There's just one thing wrong!"

"What's that?" her mother asked.

"Well, it has a cute little claw on the outside of every paw and a cute little claw on the inside of every paw – but the poor little thing has no claws at all in the middle of its paws!"

Her mother smiled. "Don't worry, Kitty . . . when you wake up on Christmas morning you'll find the claws are there."

Now Kitty loved her kitten dearly, but she worried about those claws in the middle of its paws. The days passed and there wasn't even a hint, a clue or an inkling of claws in the middle of its paws!

When Christmas Eve arrived and there was still no sign, Kitty went to her mother and asked again, "Are you absolutely *sure* that the kitten will have its middle claws tomorrow? There's only a few hours to go and there's not a hint or a clue or an inkling as to claws as far as I can see!"

"Wait till you wake up on Christmas morning," her mother smiled and went on stuffing the turkey.

So Kitty went to sleep a worried girl. And when she woke up on Christmas morning she ignored the presents in her stocking and rushed downstairs to look at her little kitten.

She was astounded, amazed and just a little surprised to see that her kitten had four claws on every paw! The middle ones had appeared as if by magic.

Kitty rushed to her parent's bedroom. "Mummy, Mummy! The kitten has grown its middle claws!"

"Of course it has," her mother grinned.

"But how did you *know*?" Kitty demanded.

Her father rolled over sleepily and sighed, "Oh, Kitty, everybody knows . . . that Centre-claws always comes at Christmas!"

ELEVEN CHRISTMAS JOKES

As I told you, Gnellie is a gnome who's always feeling poorly . . .

GNELLIE: Doctor, doctor, I keep thinking I'm a Christmas bell!

DOCTOR: Just take these pills – and, if they don't work, give me a ring!

109

GNELLIE:	Doctor, doctor, with all the excitement of Christmas I can't sleep.
DOCTOR:	Try lying on the edge of your bed . . . you'll soon drop off!
GNELLIE:	Doctor, doctor, Father Christmas gives us oranges every Christmas. Now I think I'm turning into an orange!
DOCTOR:	Have you tried playing squash?
GNELLIE:	Will that make me fit?
DOCTOR:	No. To get a gnome fit you'll have to go to an elf farm.
GNELLIE:	What else should I do?
DOCTOR:	You have to eat your greens – put a bit of colour in your cheeks!
GNELLIE:	Who wants green cheeks!
DOCTOR:	Don't worry. You'll live to be a hundred!
GNELLIE:	I was a hundred last Christmas.
DOCTOR:	There you are! What did I tell you! Now just breathe out four times.
GNELLIE:	You want to check my lungs?
DOCTOR:	No. I want to clean my glasses.
GNELLIE:	Doctor, doctor, I feel as tense as an elastic band.

DOCTOR:	Snap out of it.
GNELLIE:	It's fear of going into that little dark toy cupboard of Father Christmas'.
DOCTOR:	You're suffering from Claustrophobia.
GNELLIE:	And I keep imagining I'm a snow-covered field!
DOCTOR:	What *has* come over you?
GNELLIE:	Two sleighs, three polar bears and a flock of penguins!

GNELLIE: Doctor, doctor, I've got a bad stomach.

DOCTOR: Keep your coat buttoned up and no one will notice.

GNELLIE: But doctor, I think I need glasses!

DOCTOR: You certainly do. I'm the baker!

GNELLIE: I have bad kidneys.

DOCTOR: Then take them back – to the butcher's next door!

GNELLIE: Doctor, doctor, will this ointment cure my spots?

DOCTOR: I'm not making any rash promises.

GNELLIE:	My problem is that I keep stealing things when I go Christmas shopping. Can you give me something for it!
DOCTOR:	Try this medicine . . . and if it doesn't work come back and bring me a new video camera.
DOCTOR:	Nurse! I want to operate. Take this patient to the theatre.
GNELLIE:	Ooh! Good! I love a nice pantomime at Christmas!

Gnellie went to the doctor with a reindeer on her head.

"Gosh!" the doctor exclaimed. "You have a real problem there!"

"I certainly have!" the reindeer moaned. "Get this rotten gnome from under my feet!"

And talking about Father Christmas' reindeer you really should know their names.

GNIGEL:	What does Father Christmas call that three-legged reindeer?
GNORA:	Eileen.
GNORMAN:	And what does he call that reindeer with only one eye?
GNELLIE:	No-eye-deer!

113

GNEIL: And what do you call the reindeer with cotton wool in his ears?

GNOCKER: Call him anything you like – he won't hear you!

GNEIL: What do you call the reindeer with one eye higher than the other?

GNOCKER: Isaiah!

GNORMAN: What about the reindeer with only one eye that's got no legs?

GNELLIE: Still no-eye-deer.

GNANCY: What's the name of the reindeer with three humps on its back?

GNIGEL: Humphrey, of course.

GNANCY: And that black and blue reindeer?

GNIGEL: Bruce.

114

GNORA: Tell me, Father Christmas, how did Rudolph get that song written about him?

FATHER CHRISTMAS: Well, it's a long story . . . Once upon a time there was a king in Lapland called Rudolph. He had bright ginger hair so his people called him Rudolph the Red.

Now Rudolph the Red was bad-tempered and argued a lot. He gave his poor wife, Gertrude the Green, a terrible time. No matter what she said he had to argue.

One winter's day Gertrude the Green looked out of the palace window and said, "Oh, dear, it's snowing again. You'll have to clear the footpath before mother comes to tea."

"Humph!" Rudolph the Red grunted. He didn't fancy shifting snow and he didn't want

115

Gertrude the Green's mother coming to tea. "That's not snow. It's rain!" he argued.

"But it's white and fluffy and drifting," Gertrude the Green tried to tell him.

Rudolph the Red hid behind his newspaper and snapped, "It's rain!"

Gertrude the Green became quite angry. "Gertrude the Green knows snow, darling!"

"Yes," retorted her husband. "And Rudolph the Red knows rain, dear!"

"What a great title for a song!" Gertrude the Green exclaimed.

Of course Rudolph is the most famous of Father Christmas' reindeer. Not many people know that he's always getting lost. In fact, he was lost when Gnorman the Gnome first came across him . . .

Gnorman the Gnome went to Father Christmas and said, "Father Christmas! I've just found this red-nosed reindeer wandering around outside."

"Ah!" Father Christmas exclaimed. "Take him down to the Greenland zoo, eh Gnorman?"

And off went Gnorman.

But the next day Father Christmas saw Gnorman with the red-nosed reindeer trotting behind. "I thought I told you to take that reindeer to the zoo, Gnorman!"

"Yes, I took him yesterday," Gnorman answered. "And he liked it so much that I'm taking him to the circus today and the cinema tomorrow!"

GNELLIE:	You don't see many reindeer in zoos, do you?
GNANCY:	No. They can't afford the admission.
FATHER CHRISTMAS:	Rudolph the red-nosed reindeer's gone missing again, Gnocker. Put a "Missing" advert in the local paper!
GNOCKER:	Don't be daft. Reindeer can't read!
GNANCY:	Tell me, Gnigel, how would you get four reindeer in a car?
GNIGEL:	I don't know, Gnancy, how *would* you get four reindeer in a car?
GNANCY:	Two in the front and two in the back!
GNIGEL:	And how do you get four polar bears in a car?
GNANCY:	Take the reindeer out first.

Most people imagine that it's easy flying through the air with Father Christmas to deliver all those presents. But, if truth were told, Father Christmas is not too good a driver and we have some pretty scary times, I can tell you . . .

I remember when Father Christmas first passed his sleigh-driving test. He came skidding down in front of the toy factory.

"Have you passed?" Gneil asked.

Father Christmas pointed proudly to the front of the sleigh. "See for yourself!" he called proudly. "No-el plates!"

He was a terrible driver at first. We had a reindeer who always crashed . . . so we called him "Rex".

One snowy night Father Christmas checked the sledge. "Are my indicators working, Gnora?" he asked, flicking the switch.

"Yes – no – yes – no – yes – no – yes – no!" Gnora replied.

119

"I think I'll have to take this sledge for a service," Father Christmas sighed.

"You'd never get it up the church steps," Gnellie told him.

He'd gone no further than Greenland motorway when he broke down. He flagged down a passing motorist and asked, "Can you help me fix my sledge?"

"Sorry," the motorist replied. "I'm not a mechanic – I'm a chiropodist."

"Well, can you give me a toe?"

Now Father Christmas was late. He managed to fix his sleigh, and raced across the sky till he was stopped by a policeman in a helicopter – from the Flying Squad! "I have reason to believe you were exceeding the speed limit,"

the policeman said.

"*I* wasn't!" Father Christmas lied. "But I passed two fellers who were!"

"I'm sorry, sir," the policeman went on. "I'll have to ask you to accompany me!"

Father Christmas took a guitar from a sack and said, "Certainly, officer, what would you like to sing?"

"I'd like you to accompany me to the station," the policeman said.

"Why? Are you catching a train?"

"I mean the police station," the policeman said.

"Where's that?" Father Christmas asked.

"In the Avenue."

"Which avenue?"

"'Ello, 'ello, 'ello, let's-be avenue!"

At the police station Father Christmas was asked if he knew he was going up a one-way street.

"But I was only going one way!" he argued.

"Didn't you see the arrows?"

"Arrows! I didn't even see the Indians!"

"And what gear were you in when you hit those penguins?"

"Oh," Father Christmas told him. "The usual gear. Red suit, trimmed with white fur, and black boots!"

121

"I'll have to lock you up for the night, Father Christmas," the policeman said.

"What's the charge?"

"Oh, there's no charge. It's all part of the service!"

Father Christmas was so late delivering presents that he ran out of reindeer juice and started to crash-land.

"May-day! May-day!" Father Christmas cried into his radio. "Come in, control! I am crashing! I repeat, I am crashing!"

"Control here, control here!" came the reply. "Father Christmas, please state your height and position!"

"Er, five foot eight and about six foot behind Rudolph's bum!"

Father Christmas was late home that year. He let the reindeer back into their stalls to play . . .

GNOCKER:	What game do reindeer play in their stalls?
GNEIL:	Stable-tennis, of course!

Gnora wanted to let Rudolph into the house . . .

GNELLIE:	Keep that reindeer out of the house! It's full of fleas!
GNORA:	You'd better stay out of the house, Rudolph – it's full of fleas.

So Gnora took Rudolph back to the stalls and they pulled Christmas crackers with the world's worst jokes . . .

GNORA: What reindeer can jump higher than a house?

RUDOLPH: They all can! Houses can't jump!

GNORA: Why are Father Christmas' reindeer like a cricket match?

RUDOLPH: Because they're both stopped by the rein.

GNORA: What has antlers, pulls Father Christmas' sleigh and is made of cement?

RUDOLPH: I don't know.

GNORA: A reindeer!

RUDOLPH: What about the cement?

GNORA: I just threw that in to make it hard.

GNORA: What's the difference between a reindeer and a snowball?

RUDOLPH: They're both brown, except the snowball.

GNORA: Why don't Prancer and Dancer and the other reindeer overtake you, Rudolph?

RUDOLPH: Because they don't believe in passing the buck!

GNORA: What bird can write under the Arctic Ocean?

RUDOLPH: A ball-point pen-guin.

GNORA:	Why don't the polar bears eat the penguins?
RUDOLPH:	Because they can't get the silver paper off!
GNORA:	One Last reindeer joke, then it's your turn, Rudolph. What has antlers and loves cheese?
RUDOLPH:	Mickey Moose!
RUDOLPH:	What did the beaver say to the Christmas tree?
GNORA:	It's been nice gnawing you!

RUDOLPH:	What bird gasps and pants at the North Pole?
GNORA:	A puffin.
RUDOLPH:	How do you get milk from a polar bear?
GNORA:	Rob its fridge and run like mad.
RUDOLPH:	What do you call Christmas ducks?
GNORA:	Christmas quackers.
RUDOLPH:	And what happens when they fly upside down?
GNORA:	They quack up!
RUDOLPH:	What do you call a cow at the North Pole?
GNORA:	An eski-moo!
RUDOLPH:	I'll bet you can't tell me where my mother comes from!
GNORA:	Alaska!
RUDOLPH:	That's cheating!

ON THE TWELFTH DAY OF CHRISTMAS
MY TRUE LOVE SENT TO ME

TWELVE FATHER CHRISTMASES

When all the presents are delivered, Father Christmas likes to relax. In fact he goes to bed after Christmas and sets the alarm for Easter. And he doesn't like to be disturbed . . .

GNIGEL: Father Christmas, there's a bird at the door with a yellow bill.

FATHER CHRISTMAS: I don't care what colour its bill is, I'm not paying it!

GNORA: Father Christmas, there's a man at the door with a wooden leg!

FATHER CHRISTMAS: Tell him to hop it!

So, you see, Father Christmas is far from perfect . . .

GNORMAN: What rides a sleigh, gives lots of presents and has plenty of faults?

GNELLIE: Santa Flaws.

GNEIL: I remember when a lady wanted a new nightie for Christmas and asked Father Christmas for something cool and white.

GNOCKER: So he gave her a fridge!

GNEIL: And the time Father Christmas buried some potatoes two metres under the North Pole with a packet of razor blades.

GNOCKER: Said he was trying to grow frozen chips.

GNORMAN: What about the time when Father Christmas ran over that lady's cat? He went to her door to apologize and said, "Do you think I could replace it?"

"I don't know," the woman sniffed. "How good are you at catching mice?"

GNOCKER: Father Christmas once came down in the South Seas and had to deliver presents on the back of a huge fish.

GNEIL: An accident?

GNOCKER: No. He did it on porpoise.

GNIGEL:	Then there was the time Father Christmas lost his underpants.
GNORA:	That's how he got the name Saint Knickerless!
GNELLIE:	Is it true that Father Christmas fought for Drake against the Spanish Armada?
GNEIL:	He was certainly at Plymouth Ho-ho-ho!
GNANCY:	That reminds me. What goes Ho-squelch, Ho-squelch, Ho-squelch?
GNOCKER:	Father Christmas with snow in his wellies.
GNANCY:	And what goes Ho-squelch, Ho-squelch, Ho-squelch, BANG?
GNOCKER:	Father Christmas with snow in his wellies in a minefield!
GNANCY:	And what goes Oh! Oh! Oh?
GNOCKER:	Father Christmas walking back-wards.

Father Christmas is very easy to spot . . . fat, with snowy hair and a red suit, flying round the sky on a sleigh. But surprisingly few people see him.

GNIGEL:	A group of mountain climbers once heard Father Christmas go past.

130

GNORMAN: They must have had sharp ears!

GNIGEL: Of course. They were mountain-ears!

GNORA: Mind you, Father Christmas has tried to do something about his bald patch. He went to Doctor Weirdly to get a hair restorer. The doctor said, "I have some good news and some bad news! The bad news is that I can't make hair grow on your head . . . but the good news is that I can shrink your head so the little bit you have got fits!"

131

GNELLIE:	And of course he gets his clothes cheap.
GNEIL:	He certainly gets them for a ridiculous figure.
GNELLIE:	Did you know that Father Christmas once climbed on a "Speak-your-weight" machine?
GNEIL:	And the machine said "One at a time please!"

We gnomes can be very cruel about Father Christmas at times. Last Christmas he was asked to do a lot of television adverts. When he got back to the North Pole he asked us:

"Did you see me?"
"On and off," we said.
"And how did you like me?"
"Off!" we told him.

But Father Christmas' worst gnome is Gnigel . . .
because Gnigel is so stupid. He always has been.

GNORMAN: He thought "Illegal" was a sick bird.

GNELLIE: He thought "Backgammon" was a pig's behind.

GNEIL: He had a zebra and he called it "Spot".

GNOCKER: When he was asked to do a bird impression he ate a plate full of worms!

GNANCY: And when a cake recipe said "Separate two eggs" he put one in the kitchen and one in the bedroom.

Gnigel was trouble at school . . .

TEACHER: Gnellie, what is a comet?

GNELLIE: A star with a tail, sir.

TEACHER: Gnigel, name a comet.

GNIGEL: Er . . . Lassie, sir!

TEACHER: Unlock the piano lid, Gnigel.

GNIGEL: I can't, sir. All the keys are inside!

TEACHER: Gnigel, use the word "Gladiator" in a sentence.

GNIGEL: My chicken stopped laying eggs so I'm glad-i-ator!

TEACHER:	Gnigel. You have your wellies on the wrong feet!
GNIGEL:	They're the only feet I've got, sir!
TEACHER:	Show our guest the door, Gnigel.
GNIGEL:	It's that wooden thing over there, missus!

And Gnigel was trouble when he left school . . .

He went to work for the North Pole weather service. His first caller said, "What's the chance of a shower?"

Gnigel replied, "Fine if you have enough hot water!"

So he went to work for a glazier. The trouble was he couldn't tell putty from toothpaste. Not only did his teeth stick together but all the windows he fitted fell out!

Gnigel went to work for a forester. "What's the outside of a Christmas tree called?" the forester asked.

"Dunno," Gnigel replied.

"Bark," the forester said.

"O.K. Woof! Woof!" Gnigel went.

He tried to become a long distance swimmer. But he got halfway across the English Channel, decided he couldn't make it and swam back.

Even when he had good luck he was too daft to make the most of it . . .

One day Gnigel met a Christmas fairy in the forest. The fairy liked the look of Gnigel so she said, "Little Gnome, I grant you three wishes!"

"Ooh! I'd like a can of Coke!" Gnigel gasped.

"Your wish is my command!" the fairy said and a large can of Coke appeared in front of Gnigel. It was delicious. "What is more," the fairy said. "It is magic. Every time it empties, it fills itself up again! Now what are your next two wishes?"

"That can's brill!" Gnigel cried. "I'll have another two of those!"

He once went to the doctor. "I've got a splitting headache," he complained . . . so the doctor gave him a tube of glue.

"How long can a gnome live without a brain?" Gnigel asked.
"I don't know. How old are you?"

"I keep thinking I'm a chicken," Gnigel complained.
"I can cure that," the doctor offered.
"Oh no!" Gnigel cried. "My mother needs the eggs!"

"My mother says she has an IQ of 100," Gnigel claimed. "What's an IQ of 100?"
"A hundred gnomes like you," the doctor explained.

Gnigel took his comb to the dentist because its teeth were falling out!

Gnigel went to a mind-reader – she charged him half-price.

Then Gnigel came to work for Father Christmas . . .
The other gnomes made fun of him at first . . .

GNORMAN:	I say, I say, I say. What's stupid and sees just as well from either end?
GNEIL:	Gnigel in a blindfold!
GNIGEL:	Here. What's the idea of telling everyone I'm an idiot?
GNORMAN:	Sorry. I didn't know it was a secret.
GNIGEL:	You must think I'm a perfect fool!
GNORMAN:	Nobody's perfect . . . but you come pretty close!

Mind you, Gneil was nearly as bad . . .

One day Gnigel had the job of making toy boxes. He was hammering nails into the sides of the box . . . but Gneil noticed he was throwing half the nails away.

"Here, Gnigel, why are you throwing those nails away?"

"The heads are on the wrong end," Gnigel explained.

"Don't be stupid!" Gneil cried. "Those are for the other side!"

So Gnigel gave Father Christmas a big problem when he came to work . . .

One day Gnigel phoned Father Christmas to say he couldn't come in to work because he'd lost his voice!

One day Gnigel was very late for work. He'd been crossing a cow-meadow when his beret had blown off. He'd tried twenty on his head before he found the right one.

FATHER CHRISTMAS:	Gnigel! Call me a taxi!
GNIGEL:	You're a taxi, Father Christmas!
GNIGEL:	I've had a slight accident with your sleigh, Father Christmas!
FATHER CHRISTMAS:	Oh no! That sleigh was in mint condition!
GNIGEL:	That's all right . . . now it's a mint with a hole!
FATHER CHRISTMAS:	Gnigel, I thought I asked you to go out there and clear the snow!
GNIGEL:	I'm on my way, Father Christmas.
FATHER CHRISTMAS:	But you only have one welly on!
GNIGEL:	That's all right! There's only one foot of snow!

But generally Father Christmas and the gnomes have a merry Christmas at the North Pole . . .

Last year we all bought him a special present – guess what?

What's fat and jolly and runs on eight wheels?

Father Christmas on roller skates!

And why does Father Christmas go down chimneys?

Because they soot him.

And before you know it we are having a very happy new year . . .

Gnock! Gnock!
Who's there?
Father.
Father who?
Fa-ther sake of auld lang syne!

Then Father Christmas can sleep the rest of winter and come out in spring to tend his garden . . .

What does Father Christmas do in the summer?
Hoe, hoe, hoe!

141